NOBODY KNOWS HOW to MAKE A PIZZA

written by
Julie Borowski

illustrated by
Tetiana Kopytova

This book is inspired by Leonard Edward Read's "I, Pencil" essay. Thank you for showing us the miraculous nature of everyday things.

Believe it or not, there's not a single person on Earth who knows how to make me.

Not even the smartest person on the planet could do it.

I know what you're thinking. How can that be?
A lot of cheese pizzas are made every day all over the
world. Plus, I only have three basic ingredients: pizza
crust, tomato sauce, and cheese. I must be mistaken.

Well, let me tell you, I may look simple, but there's a lot that goes into making me! Can you believe that it took millions of people to make me?

Yup. You heard right. Millions of people to make one cheese pizza! Pretty crazy, huh?

It would take forever to tell you about everyone who played a role in making me, so let me introduce you to just a few people who helped.

Just to give you a little taste.

How to Make a Pizza

This is Farmer Leonard! He grows wheat on his farm in Texas.

Why do I need wheat? Because wheat is turned into flour, which is the main ingredient of my crust!

Farmer Leonard has special knowledge and skills. He knows things like the best time of the year to plant wheat, how much water wheat needs to grow, and how to harvest wheat.

But Farmer Leonard cannot make pizza crust on his own!
He doesn't know how to build the farm equipment, grind
the wheat into flour, or how to knead the dough.

And those are only a few of the steps that go
into making a pizza crust. There are hundreds
of other things that have to happen!

Over here is Edward! He delivers tomatoes from the farm to the factory in North Carolina.

It's a good thing Edward's here. You can't have a cheese pizza without sauce, and you can't make sauce if no one delivers the tomatoes!

Edward has special knowledge and skills. He knows how to load the truck, drive safely, and which roads to take to get to the factory.

But Edward cannot make tomato sauce on his own! He doesn't know how to grow tomatoes, cook the tomato sauce, or how to use the machines at the factory.

And those are only some of the things that need to happen!

This is Mrs. Read!

She works at the cheese factory in Wisconsin.

Mrs. Read is important. Without cheese, I wouldn't be much of a cheese pizza! I'd just be sauce on bread!

Mrs. Read's job is to cut the cheese. She has been trained to use the cutting machine to cut the cheese into perfect squares.

Mrs. Read has special skills. But she cannot make cheese on her own! She doesn't know how to milk a cow, transport the milk, or turn it into cheese.

Not to mention, all of the other things that go into making cheese!

This is Maria!

She picks lemons in Mexico.

Hey! I hear you grumbling at me. I know there are no lemons in pizza. But that doesn't mean Maria and her lemons aren't part of my story.

You see, Maria picked some of the lemons that went into the lemonade that Mrs. Read was drinking at the cheese factory.

See.

I told you there was more to me than met the eye!

Isn't it amazing how many people are involved in making one cheese pizza?

You know what's even more amazing? All these people come together to make me, but most of them are strangers to each other. They have never met.

But if they don't know each other, there must at least
be someone out there organizing them, right?
Making sure the pizza can be made?

Nope! I was created without any central planners. There was no pizza king in charge, forcing everyone to do their part. So, why did they do it?

Money!

People work for money. It's a great motivator!
The money they earn allows them to buy the things
that they want and need.

Which may be a ton of cheese pizzas!

Or not.

Did you know some people don't like pizza?

The most important thing is that everyone is free to choose what they want to do. When people have freedom, they work together to create amazing things that make the world a better place!

Made in the USA
Middletown, DE
10 November 2019